Colors: Yellow

Esther Sarfatti

Rourke
Publishing LLC
Vero Beach, Florida 32964

www.rourkepublishing.com

PHOTO CREDITS: © Nicole S. Young: title page; © Viorika Prikhodko: page 3; © Renee Brady: page 9; © Thomas Gordon: page 11; © Eric Isselée: page 13; © Tim Starkey: page 15; © Elena Aliaga: page 17; © Ariusz Nawrockis: page 19; © Marcelo Wain : page 21; © Jaroslaw Wojcik, Marcelo Wain: page 23.

Editor: Robert Stengard-Olliges

Cover design by Nicola Stratford, bdpublishing.com

Library of Congress Cataloging-in-Publication Data

Sarfatti, Esther.
  Colors : yellow / Esther Sarfatti.
      p. cm. -- (Concepts)
  ISBN 978-1-60044-520-0 (Hardcover)
  ISBN 978-1-60044-661-0 (Softcover)
  1. Colors--Juvenile literature. 2. Red--Juvenile literature. I. Title.
  QC495.5.S358 2008
  535.6--dc22
                                    2007014033

Rourke Publishing
Printed in the United States of America, North Mankato, Minnesota
091109
091109LP

Rourke Publishing

www.rourkepublishing.com – rourke@rourkepublishing.com
Post Office Box 3328, Vero Beach, FL 32964

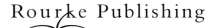

This page is yellow.

Yellow is my favorite color.

5

I like yellow flowers.

I like yellow paint.

9

STONY CREEK LIBRARY
1350 GREENFIELD PIKE
NOBLESVILLE, IN 46060

I like yellow school buses.

SCHOOL BUS

11

I like yellow birds.

13

I like yellow buckets.

I like yellow corn.

17

I like yellow chicks.

I like yellow pencils.

So many things are yellow.
Do you like yellow, too?

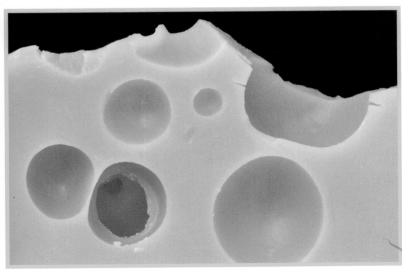

23

Index

Further Reading

Anderson, Moira, Finding Colors: *Yellow*. Heinemann, 2005.

Schuette, Sarah L. *Yellow: Seeing Yellow All Around Us*. Capstone Press, 2006.

Recommended Websites

www.enchantedlearning.com/colors/yellow.shtml

About the Author

Esther Sarfatti has worked with children's books for over 15 years as an editor and translator. This is her first series as an author. Born in Brooklyn, New York, and brought up in a trilingual home, Esther currently lives with her husband and son in Madrid, Spain.